ZOMBIE MAKERS

TRUE STORIES OF
NATURE'S UNDEAD

REBECCA L. JOHNSON

M Millbrook Press • Minneapolis

FOR THE MAD HATTER

The author would like to thank the following people for taking the time to share their insights, experiences, and expertise: Dr. David P. Hughes, Department of Entomology and Department of Biology, Penn State University, University Park, Pennsylvania; Dr. A. R. M. (Arne) Janssen, Instituut voor Biodiversiteit en Ecosysteem Dynamica, University of Amsterdam, the Netherlands; Dr. Kevin Lafferty, Channel Islands Field Station, U.S. Geological Survey Western Ecological Research Center, University of California–Santa Barbara, Santa Barbara, California; Dr. Frederic Libersat and Dr. Ram Gal, Department of Life Sciences, Ben-Gurion University, Beer-Sheva, Israel; Dr. Frédéric Thomas, Centre National de la Recherche Scientifique/Institut de Recherche pour le Développement, Montpellier, France; and Dr. Stephen P. Yanoviak, Department of Biology, University of Arkansas at Little Rock, Little Rock, Arkansas.

Milbrook Press
A division of Lerner Publishing Group, Inc.
241 First Avenue North
Minneapolis, MN 55401 U.S.A.

Website address: www.lernerbooks.com

Main type set in Caecilia LT Std 11/16.
Typeface provided by Adobe Systems.

Library of Congress Cataloging-in-Publication Data

Johnson, Rebecca L.
    Zombie makers : true stories of nature's undead / by Rebecca L. Johnson.
        p.   cm.
    Includes bibliographical references and index.
    ISBN 978–0–7613–8633–9 (lib. bdg. : alk. paper)
    ISBN 978–1–4677–0125–9 (eBook)
    1. Parasites—Juvenile literature. 2. Host-parasite relationships—Juvenile literature. I. Title.
QL757.J597 2013
578.6'5—dc23   2011046181

Manufactured in the United States of America
3 – BP – 10/1/13

ARE THEY REAL?

ZOMBIES

Does simply reading that word send chills up your spine?

That's not surprising, really. The whole idea of zombies is pretty creepy. They are dead people who have supposedly come back to life. Their minds are gone. Their bodies are decomposing. They spend a lot of time shuffling around with their arms outstretched. Mumbling and moaning. Looking for **BRAAAAIIINS** to eat. Or innocent people to turn into zombies like themselves.

Zombies on the television program Walking Dead

A person usually becomes "zombified" after being bitten by a zombie or touching its blood. It's not always clear what passes from zombie to victim to make this happen. Some sort of infection. Maybe a virus. Perhaps an alien life-form.

Once a person is infected, though, there's no hope. The zombie-making…*things*…enter the bloodstream or brain. They take control. They give the orders. And the zombie must obey.

So it's a good thing zombies aren't real, right?

Let's just say there are no zombies like those in movies or video games. Scientists know this for sure: dead people do not come back to life and start walking around, looking for trouble.

But are there…*things*…that can take over the bodies and brains of innocent creatures? Turn them into senseless slaves? Force them to create new zombies so the zombie makers can spread?

Absolutely.

And they're **closer** than you *think*.

CHAPTER 1

A FUNGUS AMONG US

ZOMBIE TRAIT #1

Stares vacantly ahead. Moves slowly and mechanically. Behaves oddly.

A garbage can tipped over. Trash is all over the ground. There's part of a hamburger. A gooey candy wrapper. A mushy apple. It's pretty disgusting. But it's a feast for the hungry flies buzzing around.

One fly, though, doesn't seem interested in the food. It walks right past, staring straight ahead. That's right—it's walking, not flying as flies usually do. The fly's movements are jerky and slow.

It's as if the fly doesn't want to move, but something is forcing it to.

That something is a fungus scientists call *Entomophthora muscae* (ent-uh-MAHF-thor-uh MUSK-eye), or *E. muscae* for short. *E. muscae* is a parasite. Parasites invade the bodies of other living things. Those living things become the parasites' hosts. Flies are the hosts of the *E. muscae* fungus. When the fungus invades, it turns normal flies into zombies.

A few days ago, an *E. muscae* spore landed on the fly. A spore is like a miniature seed, no larger than a speck of dust. Tough strands of fungus grew out of the spore. They bored through the fly's skin. The fungus spread through the fly's body, feeding on its organs and tissues. This weakened the fly. Not enough to kill it, though. Not yet.

The fungus then released chemicals into the fly's brain. The chemicals changed the fly's behavior. They turned it into a zombie with no will of its own, a creature that will do whatever the fungus commands.

Why does *E. muscae* need a zombie fly? The fungus uses the fly as food. As the fungus digests the

The life of a housefly (top) will never be the same after it encounters fly-enslaver fungus E. muscae (bottom).

ZOMBIE MAKER:
THE FUNGUS ENTOMOPHTHORA MUSCAE

NICKNAME:
FLY ENSLAVER

ZOMBIE VICTIM:
HOUSEFLIES (MUSCA DOMESTICA)

LOCATION:
NORTH AMERICA AND EUROPE

fly's insides, it gets the energy it needs to grow, make spores, and reproduce. The fungus also uses the fly to help infect more flies with spores and so spread the fungus from place to place.

The zombie fly keeps walking. It reaches a clump of tall grass near the garbage can. The fly grabs a blade of grass and climbs. Step by step, the zombie makes its way to the top.

The grass sways in the breeze. The fly grips tightly with its legs to hang on. It spreads its wings. It raises its belly, or abdomen, which is swollen from the growing mass of fungus inside. Like a statue, the fly holds this rigid, stretched-out position.

The fungus is now where it needs to be. It's high above a place where other flies are gathered. It doesn't need its zombie anymore. So the fungus destroys what's left of the fly's organs, including its brain. Soon the fly is dead.

A few hours later, little stalks of fungus grow out of the dead fly. They form a furry coating on the corpse, especially on the bloated abdomen. Each stalk holds a single spore. Each spore has the potential to infect another fly and grow into another *E. muscae* fungus.

When the spores are ripe, they shoot into the air. Then they slowly drift down. Spores land on everything below the dead fly. They land on the garbage and on the garbage-eating flies.

Spores will stick to some of those flies. A new generation of *E. muscae* fungus will begin to grow.

E. muscae has destroyed this housefly. The fungus grew mostly inside the fly while it was still alive. Once the fly died, the fungus emerged to produce spores.

Thousands of dustlike E. muscae spores surround this fly's corpse. Any spores that land on other flies will infect them, continuing the zombie-making cycle.

BODY-SNATCHER *INVASION*

Camponotus leonardi carpenter ants live in the rain forests of Southeast Asia. The ants build nests in the treetops, high above the ground. They hunt for food among the branches. Sometimes the search for food takes carpenter ants down to the forest floor. It can be a dangerous trip. *Ophiocordyceps unilateralis* (oh-fee-oh-CORD-uh-seps you-nuh-lat-er-RAL-uhs) lurks near the ground. *O. unilateralis* is another zombie-making fungus. Carpenter ants are its host.

ZOMBIE MAKER:
THE FUNGUS OPHIOCORDYCEPS UNILATERALIS

NICKNAME:
BODY SNATCHER

ZOMBIE VICTIM:
A TYPE OF CARPENTER ANT (CAMPONOTUS LEONARDI)

LOCATION:
SOUTHEAST ASIA

A carpenter ant that ventures down to the forest floor risks meeting body-snatcher fungus **O. unilateralis** *(white strands, left).*

Like *E. muscae, O. unilateralis* begins its life cycle as a spore. A spore that lands on a carpenter ant quickly sprouts. The fungus invades the ant's body. It digests the ant's insides, bit by bit.

The infected ant is back at the ant nest by the time the fungus takes over its brain.

But the nest is up in the treetops where it's hot and dry. To grow well and reproduce, O. unilateralis needs a place that is cool, shady, and damp.

O. unilateralis releases chemicals that affect the brain of its ant host. The infected ant starts to behave strangely. It twitches and stumbles, again and again. Sooner or later, the ant loses its grip and falls off the tree. Down on the ground, the ant continues twitching and stumbling. It tries climbing back up the tree but falls before it gets very high. The ant ends up clambering through low-growing plants on the forest floor. It moves in and out of the leaves as if it's searching for something.

The ant isn't actually searching, though. The fungus is. It's looking for just the right place to grow—like a driver in a car, scouting out the perfect parking spot. Eventually the fungus makes the zombie ant stop on the underside of a leaf where it's cool, shady, and damp.

At first, an infected ant acts like its nest mates. But soon its behavior changes as the fungus takes control.

A fungus stalk with a ball-like structure full of spores grows out of the dead ant's head.

The ant obeys one final command from its master. The ant opens its jaws and bites into the leaf. Then it dies. But its jaws stay clamped, anchoring it securely in place.

The fungus keeps growing inside the ant's corpse. Several days later, a long, skinny stalk erupts through the dead ant's head. After a few weeks, part of the stalk swells as spores inside develop. Ripe spores shower down onto the forest floor. Carpenter ants that walk into this spore-infested area are very likely to become infected with *O. unilateralis*. And so the zombie-making cycle will begin again.

THE SCIENCE BEHIND THE STORY

Scientists David Hughes from Penn State University and Sandra Andersen from the University of Copenhagen, Denmark, study *O. unilateralis*-infected carpenter ants in Thailand's jungles. They discovered that infected ants are almost always about 10 inches (25 centimeters) above the forest floor when they bite down on leaves. The air just above the ground is very damp, with about 95 percent humidity. The location is also fairly cool (compared to the treetops), with a temperature between 68 and 86°F (20 and 30°C). These conditions are just what *O. unilateralis* needs to grow well and produce spores.

"The fungus is a puppet master pulling the strings of the poor infected ants, making them travel a long way during the last hours of their lives to eventually die where the parasite prefers to be," said Hughes.

When the scientists examined infected carpenter ants under a microscope, they discovered that *O. unilateralis* does something else quite amazing. The fungus changes the ant's jaw muscles in a way that actually makes them more powerful when the ant bites into the leaf. And the ant's jaws remain locked, even after it dies. These changes help make sure that the ant's corpse—and the fungus inside it—won't fall off the leaf before the spores are released.

CHAPTER 2

THE WORMS CRAWL IN, THE WORMS CRAWL OUT

ZOMBIE TRAIT #2

Obeys commands without question. Will even die trying.

The sun sets on a warm summer night, and darkness closes in. A moth flutters by. Overhead, a bat swoops and dives.

Along with the normal night sounds, there's a faint rustling in the grass. Something is moving…scuffing…shuffling along. It's getting closer. Louder too.

There must be more than one.

The first few step out of the shadows and into the light. More are coming behind them. They're relentless. They're determined. Nothing can stop them.

The zombie crickets are here.

Their story began with a meal. Many weeks before, the crickets snacked on dead insects. (It's something crickets do.) Those insects had begun their lives in a lake or a stream. While in the water, they were infected by tiny young forms, or larvae, of zombie-making hairworms. The hairworms' scientific name is *Paragordius tricuspidatus* (pair-uh-GOR-dee-uhs try-kus-pih-DAH-tuhs).

The hairworm larvae didn't hurt the insects they infected. They just curled up to form little balls, called cysts, inside them. The larvae waited as cysts until the insects died and were eaten by crickets. Crickets are hairworms' true hosts.

Once inside crickets, the larvae became active. They started nibbling on their hosts' tissues. The worms grew and grew until they were nearly 3 feet (1 meter) long. Each worm looped and coiled and knotted itself up to fit inside the body of its cricket host.

The worms got restless when fully grown. They were adults and ready to reproduce. To do that, though, they needed water. The time had come for the worms to turn their hosts into zombies. The worms did the deed by releasing chemicals, which gently oozed into cricket brains.

A cricket (top) infected with the hairworm *P. tricuspidatus* (bottom) appears to live a normal life until the day the hairworm instructs the cricket to throw itself into a body of water.

ZOMBIE MAKER:
THE HAIRWORM *PARAGORDIUS TRICUSPIDATUS*

NICKNAME:
SUICIDE WORM

ZOMBIE VICTIM:
CRICKETS (*NEMOBIUS SYLVESTRIS*)

LOCATION:
EUROPE. OTHER TYPES OF HAIRWORMS ZOMBIFY VARIOUS INSECTS ON EVERY CONTINENT EXCEPT ANTARCTICA.

So now the crickets are coming, making their way toward a pond. Crickets usually avoid water. That's because crickets can't swim. Jumping in to a pond or stream would be suicide.

Controlled by their worm masters, though, these zombie crickets can do nothing else. Some hurl themselves into the water when they reach the pond. Others simply stroll in. Either way, the outcome is the same: crickets splash and thrash, and then they drown.

The hairworms quickly wriggle out of their dead or dying hosts. It's not a pretty sight. Free of the zombies they created, the worms swim off. They will mate and lay eggs. The eggs will hatch into larvae that will someday infect crickets of their own.

THE SCIENCE BEHIND THE STORY

How do hairworms get their cricket hosts to drown themselves? The chemicals the worms produce interfere with the crickets' nervous systems. They even appear to change the structure of the crickets' brains. The result is crickets that wander around until they find water. Then they are suddenly eager to get wet.

For two summers, French scientist Frédéric Thomas and his colleagues spent nearly every night watching crickets at an outdoor swimming pool near the city of Montpellier in southern France. The crickets came out of a forest near the pool soon after dark. Almost all the crickets that ended up in the water were infected with *P. tricuspidatus*. (The scientists confirmed the crickets were infected by watching the hairworms squirm out.) As part of their experiments, the scientists rescued some of the crickets the moment they hit the water. They put them back on dry ground. In every case, the rescued crickets immediately returned to the edge of the pool and jumped into the water again!

After the cricket hits the water, the 3-foot-long (1 m) hairworm wriggles out while its host drowns.

SKIN-DEEP *CREEP*

Imagine having worms living inside you. Just under your skin. So close to the surface you can see them moving around.

This nightmare is real. It's called guinea worm disease.

A parasitic worm scientists know as *Dracunculus medinensis* (drah-KUNK-you-luhs med-ih-NEN-sihs) causes the disease.

ZOMBIE MAKER:
GUINEA WORM *DRACUNCULUS MEDINENSIS*

NICKNAME:
FIERY SERPENT

ZOMBIE VICTIM:
PEOPLE *(HOMO SAPIENS)*

LOCATION:
AFRICA

Guinea worms (left) infect humans (right) who drink water containing D. medinensis larvae.

A guinea worm infection starts when a person drinks water containing tiny crustaceans, called water fleas, that are full of *D. medinensis* larvae. The larvae then break out of the water fleas and infect their human host.

Guinea worms aren't like hairworms. They don't turn people into mindless zombies eager to drown themselves.

But guinea worms *do* make people act in a way that helps the worm reproduce.

A person who has swallowed water containing *D. medinensis* larvae doesn't know anything is wrong at first. After the larvae reach the person's stomach, they move into surrounding tissues. There, they slowly grow into adults. Male and female worms mate, and the male worms die.

The females survive, though. And about a year after the infection began, they start to move.

A female guinea worm can be nearly 3 feet (1 m) long when she begins traveling through her host. She looks like a piece of long, thin spaghetti. The worm burrows through the tissues beneath the skin. She usually heads for her host's legs or feet.

The worm's body is packed with eggs. During her journey, larvae hatch from the eggs. They stay inside their mother.

When the worm is ready to emerge, she releases chemicals. The chemicals cause a large blister to form on the person's skin. The blister soon bursts, leaving a terrible sore. The tip of the worm's head is visible in the middle of the sore. But before she'll come out, one more thing needs to happen.

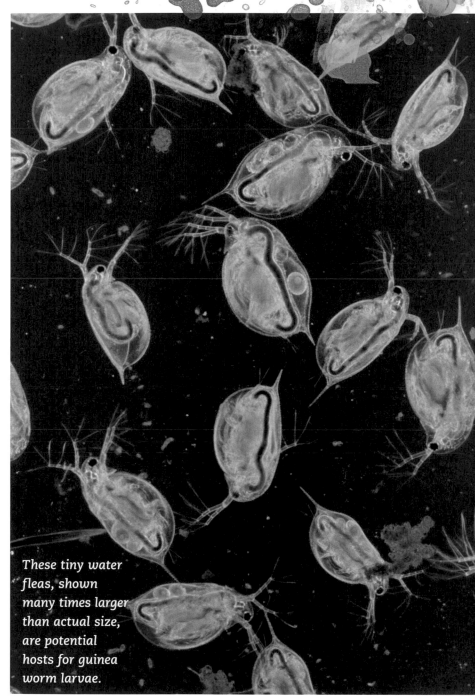

These tiny water fleas, shown many times larger than actual size, are potential hosts for guinea worm larvae.

The skin around the sore burns as if it's on fire. No one can stand the pain for very long. Driven by the pain—but really by the parasite—an infected person often heads for a lake or a stream. Plunging the sore into cool water is the only thing that makes it feel better.

The moment the sore gets wet, the guinea worm comes out. She wriggles free, releasing millions of larvae into the water as she dies. Water fleas swoop in to eat them.

If people drink this water, they'll swallow the water fleas and the larvae they contain. The guinea worm life cycle will be complete. Another round of infection will begin.

That's been the story for thousands of years. But happily, the story is changing.

A doctor has partially extracted this guinea worm from a patient's leg. This is a slow, painful process.

THE SCIENCE BEHIND THE STORY

Call it a worm war. People are battling to end guinea worm disease, and they're winning. In 1986 more than 3.5 million people in Africa and Asia were infected with guinea worm disease. The only medical treatment was to try to pull the worm out slowly and carefully. People often did this by wrapping the end of the worm around a small stick. Every day, they turned the stick a little bit and eased out a little more of the worm. Getting the whole worm out often took days, sometimes weeks. It was dangerous to hurry. If the worm broke, the part left inside could lead to infection, crippling, and even death.

But in 1986, a worldwide campaign to wipe out guinea worms began. The secret weapon? Water filters! Passing water through filters traps water fleas and the worm larvae inside them. If guinea worms can't get into their human hosts, they can't reproduce. Thanks to the use of water filters, guinea worms have been gradually dying out.

At the end of 2011, there were only about one thousand cases of guinea worm disease reported, and all were in one small region of Africa. Scientists hope that in the next few years guinea worms will die out completely, leaving the world guinea worm free.

A health official in Niger, West Africa, helps a woman filter water to prevent guinea worm disease.

CHAPTER 3

CAN WE EAT THE BABYSITTER?

ZOMBIE TRAIT #3

Doesn't respond to pain. Ignores injuries or loss of body parts. Doesn't seem to mind being eaten.

A cockroach can't make wishes. If this roach could, though, it might be wishing that it had stayed hidden. Or had taken a different path. Or that the slender green jewel wasp had flown right on by.

She didn't, though. She spotted the cockroach and turned it into a zombie with remarkable speed.

Now, try as it might, the cockroach can't run away. Its legs aren't injured. But it can't seem to make them move. Even when the wasp bites off part of the roach's antenna, the roach just stands there.

The wasp grips the antenna stump in her strong jaws. She tugs and the cockroach follows like a dog on a leash. She heads for a hole in the rocks. It's the entrance to her den.

The cockroach follows its zombie master into that small dark space.

But it won't come out again.

The attack happened so quickly. The jewel wasp swooped down and jabbed her stinger into the cockroach's neck. The roach's front legs buckled. They were instantly paralyzed.

Unable to escape, the roach lay there while the wasp probed its brain with her stinger. It took her a minute or two to find just the right spot. Then she jabbed the stinger in hard to release a stream of venom.

The venom interfered with normal processes in that part of the cockroach's brain. The venom made it impossible for the cockroach to *start* walking on its own. Even after the first sting wore off and the cockroach's front legs were no longer paralyzed, it couldn't take a step.

For the cockroach, life as a zombie had just begun. And the wasp? She had just created the perfect babysitter.

After stinging the cockroach, the wasp prepares to lead it to her den.

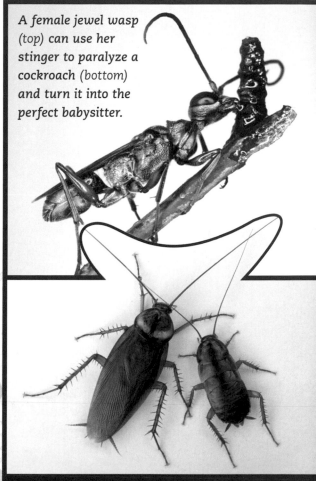

A female jewel wasp (top) can use her stinger to paralyze a cockroach (bottom) and turn it into the perfect babysitter.

ZOMBIE MAKER:
THE JEWEL WASP AMPULEX COMPRESSA

NICKNAME:
COCKROACH TAMER

ZOMBIE VICTIM:
COCKROACHES (PERIPLANETA AMERICANA)

LOCATION:
TROPICAL PARTS OF AFRICA, SOUTH ASIA, AND THE PACIFIC ISLANDS

23

A young jewel wasp emerges from the dead body of its former babysitter.

Now the cockroach stands quietly inside the den. It doesn't move as the wasp lays an egg on its body. The roach can only watch as she blocks the den's entrance with pebbles on her way out.

There in the darkness, the cockroach waits.

Two days later, a wormlike larva hatches from the egg. It chews a hole in the roach's body and sips its blood. Then it wriggles inside and eats the roach's organs. Not all at once. It eats them slowly, one by one. The meal lasts about a week. The cockroach stays alive until the very end.

Inside the roach's half-empty corpse, the plump larva spins a cocoon. It enters the pupal stage of its life cycle, when a larva becomes an adult.

Four weeks later, the transformation is complete. A young jewel wasp claws its way out of what's left of its babysitter. The wasp pushes aside the pebbles blocking the den's entrance. With a flash of green, it's gone.

THE SCIENCE BEHIND THE STORY

Scientists Frederic Libersat and Ram Gal from Israel's Ben-Gurion University study how jewel wasps create zombie cockroaches. They've discovered that venom from the wasp's second sting affects only a specific part of the cockroach's brain. It targets a bundle of nerves that control walking movements. If the scientists inject the venom into other parts of a cockroach's brain, it has no effect at all.

How does the wasp find this special spot? The two scientists solved this mystery by looking closely at the wasp's stinger. They used an electron microscope to see the tip in great detail. The stinger's tip has unusual structures that the scientists believe are sensors. They think the wasp uses these sensors to "feel" her way around inside a cockroach's head. The sensors let her know when she's hit the right spot to inject her zombie-making venom.

CONTROL FREAKS

The caterpillar looks like a Ninja warrior. Every muscle in its body is tensed. With head held high and front legs poised, the caterpillar is ready to fight. It will take on any attacker that tries to harm the cocoons.

The cocoons are clustered at the tip of a branch. Each cocoon holds a small wasp larva, wrapped in strands of baby-soft silk. The larvae are helpless at this point in their lives, as they slowly change into adults.

ZOMBIE MAKER:
THE PARASITOID WASP
GLYPTAPANTELES SPP.

NICKNAME:
BODYGUARD CREATOR

ZOMBIE VICTIM:
MOTH CATERPILLARS
(THYRINTEINA LEUCOCERAE)

LOCATION:
NORTH AND SOUTH
AMERICA

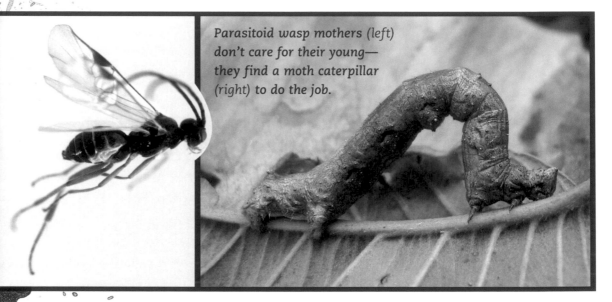

Parasitoid wasp mothers (left) don't care for their young— they find a moth caterpillar (right) to do the job.

A hungry stinkbug smells the larvae. They would make a fine dinner. The bug creeps toward the caterpillar that's silently standing guard. Then the bug rushes forward and tries to push past.

The caterpillar explodes into action. It lashes out with a hard body blow and sends the stinkbug soaring.

Score one for the zombie bodyguard.

How did a caterpillar come to have such a job? The story started weeks ago. A little *Glyptapanteles* (glip-tuh-pan-TEL-eez) wasp spotted the caterpillar. The wasp landed softly on the caterpillar's back and began laying eggs. She didn't lay them *on* the caterpillar, though. The wasp injected the eggs into the caterpillar's body. She used a stingerlike structure to puncture the caterpillar's tough skin.

Wiggly wasp larvae hatched from the eggs. The caterpillar wasn't bothered too much by this. It kept behaving normally, crawling around and munching on leaves.

Inside their host, the wasp larvae crawled around too. They snacked on the caterpillar's tissues. They sipped its pale, watery blood.

The caterpillar was still acting normally when the larvae gnawed holes in its body. It did twitch a bit when they squirmed through its skin.

A caterpillar lies quietly as the wasp larvae crawl out of it.

The caterpillar really changed, though, when the larvae settled on the branch and spun their cocoons. The caterpillar reared up on its hind legs. It leaned protectively over the white silken bundles. It became what the larvae needed most: a strong zombie guardian with one goal. *Protect ... the ... cocoons.*

A zombie caterpillar stands guard over the wasp cocoons in its care.

The caterpillar resumes its martial arts pose, now that the stinkbug is gone. Each time danger threatens, though, the caterpillar does the same thing. It thrashes back and forth to drive would-be attackers away.

The caterpillar has been on guard duty for many days. It hasn't eaten during that time. It can't last much longer.

So it's a good thing, then, that its assignment is almost over. The cocoons are twitching. The young wasps inside are ready to come out. Thanks to their zombie protector, they have survived the change from larvae to adults.

By this time tomorrow, the young wasps will be gone.

And their bodyguard will be dead.

THE SCIENCE BEHIND THE STORY

Dutch scientists Arne Janssen and Amir Grosman have studied zombie caterpillars in Brazil for several years. One of the questions they wanted to answer was what controls the caterpillars and forces them to stand guard. Is it the female wasp? The larvae? Or the young wasps developing inside the cocoons?

The female wasp didn't seem a likely choice. After laying her eggs, she leaves, never to return. The larvae didn't seem to be the controllers, either. All the time they were inside the caterpillar, it behaved in a fairly normal way.

Suspicion fell on the young wasps developing inside the cocoons. So the scientists separated the caterpillars from the cocoons they were guarding. To their surprise, the caterpillars stayed zombified!

The scientists were baffled. And then—a clue. Inside every caterpillar, they found one or two wasp larvae. These larvae had stayed behind when the others crawled out of the caterpillar's body. Could these larvae be the zombie makers? Could they be controlling the bodyguard, making it watch over the cocoons? The scientists think these stay-behind larvae may release chemicals that affect the caterpillar's brain. If so, these larvae sacrifice themselves so the others will have a better chance of surviving.

Do these stay-behind larvae also kill the bodyguard when their brothers and sisters have changed into wasps?

"It is not known what kills the caterpillar," says Janssen, "but it may be weakened by the lack of food, and of course, it has been fed upon by the wasp larvae. It is intriguing that the time of death seems to be always after the adult wasps have emerged from their cocoons, when they do not need a bodyguard anymore."

CHAPTER 4
GOING VIRAL

ZOMBIE TRAIT #4

Goes insane.
Tries to bite and infect others.

A raccoon paces beside a stream deep in the woods. The raccoon's steps are jumpy and jerky, as though it's walking on hot coals. Chattering and whining, the raccoon snaps at the air. There's nothing there, though. Not even a fly.

The raccoon sits back on its haunches. It stares at the water and whimpers. Frothy saliva runs out between its lips and drips on the ground. The raccoon edges closer to the water. Body quivering, it dips its head to drink. But it growls and jerks back the moment its mouth touches the water. Furious, the raccoon sprints away and collides with a tree. It whirls around, savagely hissing and snarling.

It bites at the tree bark, again and again.

A bite started all this madness.

The raccoon spotted something small and dark along the edge of a country road. Maybe it was food, tossed from a passing car. The raccoon scuttled over to investigate. It sniffed at the lump and flipped it over. The lump was a bat, close to death. With a high-pitched hiss, the dying bat sank its teeth into the raccoon's paw.

The bat's saliva was teeming with viruses that cause the disease rabies. Some of these viruses got into the wound on the raccoon's paw. That was all it took for the infection to begin and rabies to develop.

The viruses multiplied. A dozen became a hundred. Then a thousand. Then a million. The viruses traveled along the raccoon's nerves and spread throughout its body. They collected in the salivary glands in the raccoon's mouth. After a few weeks, the raccoon's saliva was thick with viruses, just as the bat's had been.

The viruses also invaded the raccoon's brain. They swarmed into the parts of the brain that control behavior. As they damaged these parts, the raccoon showed symptoms of rabies. It grew irritable. Then aggressive. Then crazed. With the growing madness came a growing urge—the desperate need to bite.

The rabies virus (top) can infect many different animals, including raccoons (bottom) and humans.

ZOMBIE MAKER:
THE RABIES VIRUS, A TYPE OF *LYSSAVIRUS*

NICKNAME:
MAD DOG DISEASE

ZOMBIE VICTIM:
MAMMALS (MOSTLY RACCOONS, SKUNKS, BATS, AND FOXES)

LOCATION:
EVERY COUNTRY EXCEPT AUSTRALIA AND NEW ZEALAND

Many animals sick with rabies have an uncontrollable urge to bite anything that comes within reach.

The raccoon lurches out of the trees. It's limping. The virus is damaging nerves all over its body. One of its back legs has gone numb. The other one is twitching. The raccoon is very sick now. Like the bat that bit it days ago, it's dying.

A big white house sits back from the road. A long driveway leads up to it. Cattle graze in a pasture beyond the house.

A screen door slams. A dog starts barking.

The raccoon growls at the noise. The need to bite gets stronger.

The dog barks again. The raccoon snarls and heads toward the sound.

THE SCIENCE BEHIND THE STORY

The rabies virus can turn a normal animal into a furious, crazed being with an uncontrollable urge to bite. A rabid animal's saliva is teeming with viruses. One deep bite is usually all it takes to spread the infection to a new host.

Many kinds of animals, including people, can get rabies. The disease is nearly always fatal and a nasty way to die. Fortunately, there's a vaccine for rabies. The vaccine doesn't cure the disease. It helps the body kill the viruses and so prevents the deadly infection from developing.

French scientist and chemist Louis Pasteur created the first rabies vaccine in the 1880s. In 1885 Pasteur tried it out on Joseph Meister, a nine-year-old boy who'd been bitten by a rabid dog. Pasteur had tested his vaccine on animals. But he'd never used it successfully on a person. He gave Meister a daily injection of his rabies vaccine for thirteen days. The boy didn't develop rabies. The success of the vaccine made Pasteur a national hero.

Most children in the United States are given vaccines to prevent diseases such as measles, mumps, and whooping cough. Many people get a yearly flu shot, a vaccine to prevent influenza (flu). The rabies vaccine isn't one you'd probably get unless you were bitten by an animal suspected of having rabies. If you ever do need the vaccine, speed is key. You'd need to get it within twelve to forty-eight hours of being bitten to stop the virus and prevent the disease.

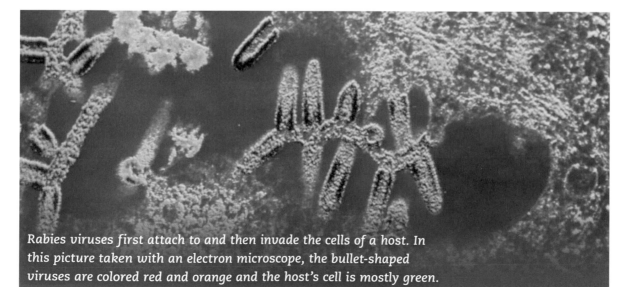

Rabies viruses first attach to and then invade the cells of a host. In this picture taken with an electron microscope, the bullet-shaped viruses are colored red and orange and the host's cell is mostly green.

CHAPTER 5

TRY ME, YOU'LL LIKE ME

ZOMBIE TRAIT #5

Tricks victims into becoming infected so they will spread the zombifying factor.

Splat! A bird dropping lands on a leaf. A giant gliding ant (named for its ability to control how it falls if it tumbles off a tree) soon discovers it. Gliding ants live in the treetops. Bird droppings are one of the things they eat. Bird droppings are usually full of tasty things. Like bits of lizard skin. Insect legs. Tiny seeds from rain forest fruits.

This bird dropping has a little something extra. It's full of microscopic eggs belonging to Myrmeconema neotropicum (muhr-meh-koh-NEE-mah nee-oh-TRAH-pick-um).

These are the eggs of a zombie-making worm.

The gliding ant scoops up some of the bird dropping in its jaws. It carries it back to its treetop nest. There, the egg-infested food is served to a few ant larvae in the nest's nursery. And so the making of ant zombies begins.

Tiny male and female worms hatch from the eggs. The worms grow for a while inside their young hosts. Then they mate, and the female worms start laying eggs.

By the time the ant larvae have become young ants, their gasters—the back part of their abdomens—are crammed with M. *neotropicum* eggs. Each infected ant's gaster gradually turns from jet black to bright red. From a distance, this big, round backside looks like a plump red berry. In fact, it looks just like the red berries on some rain forest plants.

M. *neotropicum* caused this color change. It has somehow made the ants behave differently too. Normal giant gliding ants keep to the shadows as they scurry around looking for food. Infected ants stroll around in plain sight, holding their red gasters high.

Birds don't usually eat giant gliding ants. The ants have nasty spines. But birds are easily fooled by these ant zombies. They mistake the ants' red backsides for berries.

Getting eaten by a bird is the end of the story for an M. *neotropicum*-infected ant. But what about the worm eggs inside it? They'll survive the trip through the bird's digestive tract. The eggs will leave the bird's body in its droppings. Chances are, some of those droppings will land near another nest of giant gliding ants, who'll be tempted to make them a meal.

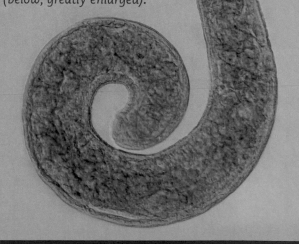

Giant gliding ants (top) are hosts for M. neotropicum, a minute zombie-making worm (below, greatly enlarged).

ZOMBIE MAKER:
THE ROUNDWORM MYRMECONEMA NEOTROPICUM

NICKNAME:
BERRY MAKER

ZOMBIE VICTIM:
GIANT GLIDING ANTS (CEPHALOTES ATRATUS)

LOCATION:
RAIN FORESTS OF CENTRAL AND SOUTH AMERICA

35

The red, egg-packed gasters of infected giant gliding ants resemble some types of rain forest berries.

THE SCIENCE BEHIND THE STORY

In 2005 American scientists Steve Yanoviak, Michael Kaspari, and Robert Dudley were studying giant gliding ants in Panama. Near one ant nest, they spotted several ants with bright red gasters. They collected the ants and returned to their laboratory for a closer look.

Kaspari thought the red-gastered ants might be a new species of *Cephalotes*. Dudley didn't think so, and the two men made a bet. Then Yanoviak dissected one of the ants under a microscope. Its gaster was packed with hundreds of parasitic worm eggs.

"I think the most exciting moment was when I first opened the gaster of a 'berry' ant and a bunch of eggs poured out," Yanoviak said. "After that, the questions just started flowing."

The scientists realized the red-gastered ants weren't a new species. (Kaspari lost the bet.) They were *Cephalotes atratus* ants that had been changed by a parasitic worm.

The worm, it turned out, *was* a new species. It was given the scientific name *Myrmeconema neotropicum* by George Poinar Jr., another scientist involved in the project. This zombie-making parasite is the first one known to science that makes part of its host look like fruit.

DINNER DISGUISE

Last week, the snail would never have left the cool safety of the shadows. It would have stayed hidden among the garden plants. If danger threatened, the snail would have pulled in the slender, dark tentacles on its head. It would have crouched beneath its shell and waited for the danger to pass. But today, everything is different.

ZOMBIE MAKER:
THE FLATWORM *LEUCOCHLORIDIUM PARADOXUM*

NICKNAME
GREEN-BANDED BROODSAC

ZOMBIE VICTIM
AMBER SNAILS (*SUCCINEA PUTRIS*)

LOCATION
UNITED KINGDOM, EUROPE, WESTERN AND NORTHERN ASIA

The flatworm L. paradoxum (inside tentacle, right) changes amber snails (left) from timid shade dwellers into sun worshipers.

Today, the snail doesn't hesitate to crawl out into the open. The sunny tips of the leaves seem inviting.

Today, when danger threatens, the snail doesn't pull its tentacles into its head. It can't. Its tentacles are no longer slender and dark. They are fat and bulging. They are striped green and white. And they are twisting, twitching, and pulsing in a most unsettling way.

Actually, it's the things inside the tentacles that are moving.

The tentacles of an infected snail resemble juicy, wriggling caterpillars. Mmmm... delicious!

They are the larvae of a zombie-making worm called *Leucochloridium paradoxum* (loo-koh-klor-RID-ee-um pair-uh-DAHK-sum). The worm needs two hosts to complete its life cycle. Birds are one. Amber snails are the other.

The adult worms live in the digestive tracts of small birds. The worms don't harm the birds. They simply produce lots of eggs that get spread around in the birds' droppings.

Like giant gliding ants, amber snails eat bird droppings. If a snail eats *L. paradoxum*-infected droppings, it gets a bellyful of eggs. Worm larvae hatch from the eggs. They go through several stages inside the snail. Eventually, the larvae invade the tentacles on the snail's head.

And there, the larvae work a sort of magic. They turn the snail's tentacles into what look like plump, juicy, and very lively caterpillars.

The larvae also take control of the snail's small and simple brain. They make their zombie snail do things a normal snail never would. It crawls out into the open, often climbing to the tops of leaves. It sits in these exposed places, with its tentacles pulsing.

It doesn't take long for hungry birds to notice. Once a bird spots the "caterpillars," it can't resist. The bird snips off the snail's twitching tentacles and gulps them down. The parasite has just moved to the bird phase of its life cycle again, thanks to its disguise—and its zombie host.

The snail may live for some time longer, but its life will never be the same.

BRAIN *TEASERS*

Cats eat rats. So it's no surprise that rats are afraid of cats. But rats infected with *Toxoplasma gondii* (tahk-soh-PLAZ-muh GAHN-dee) aren't. They'll walk right up to a cat and try to be friends. They do it because they've been zombified.

T. gondii is a one-celled, parasitic protozoan, too small to see with the naked eye. The parasite spends part of its life cycle inside cats. It doesn't turn cats into zombies. It simply lays eggs inside them. The eggs pass out of the cat's digestive tract.

ZOMBIE MAKER:
THE SINGLE-CELLED PARASITE
TOXOPLASMA GONDII

NICKNAME:
RAT CONTROLLER

ZOMBIE VICTIM:
RATS AND OTHER WARM-
BLOODED ANIMALS

LOCATION:
EVERYWHERE CATS ARE FOUND

A rat (left) infected with T. gondii (right) loses all fear of cats, which doesn't bode well for the rat.

T. gondii spends the second part of its life cycle in some other warm-blooded animal. This second host is typically a rat. Rats will eat almost anything. When a rat nibbles the waste of an infected cat, it swallows millions of eggs. The eggs hatch. The parasites invade. Many head for the rat's brain.

They zero in on the part of the brain that controls fear.

When a cat eats an infected rat, the parasite enters the cat, where it can then lay its eggs.

There, the parasites release chemicals that somehow turn off the rat's fear of cats. What's more, the chemicals make the rat attracted to the odor of cats. One whiff and it wants to be near them.

A rat that strolls up to a cat will very likely get eaten. Bad for the rat. But good for the parasite. By making rats into zombies, *T. gondii* improves its chances of moving from cats to rats and back to cats again.

THE SCIENCE BEHIND THE STORY

Rats are usually *T. gondii*'s second host. But the parasite can infect almost any warm-blooded animal including birds, dogs, and cows. It can also infect humans.

People usually become infected with *T. gondii* by eating undercooked meat. But they can also get it from eating unwashed vegetables grown in soil that's contaminated with the parasite. Or cleaning litter boxes used by infected cats. In fact, people can pick up the parasite in all sorts of ways.

If a pregnant woman becomes infected with *T. gondii*, her baby might be harmed. *T. gondii* can also harm people who are already ill with certain diseases. But millions of perfectly healthy people around the world have this parasite in their brains. And it doesn't affect them at all.

At least, that's what scientists used to think. Recent studies show something else. *T. gondii* may slightly change people's personalities. For instance, people infected with the parasite seem to be more willing to take risks than people who aren't.

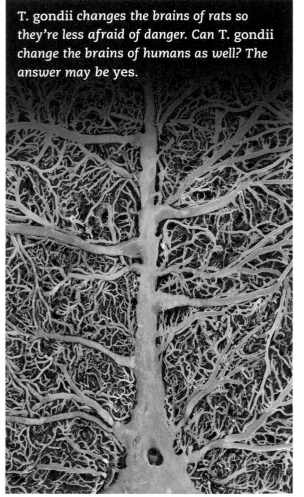

T. gondii changes the brains of rats so they're less afraid of danger. Can T. gondii change the brains of humans as well? The answer may be yes.

Is *T. gondii* trying to do in people what it does in rats? Make them less afraid of danger? At this point, scientists aren't sure. "The effects of *T. gondii* are subtle—too subtle to easily notice. And we still don't fully understand them," says Kevin Lafferty, a scientist with the U.S. Geological Survey who studies brain-changing parasites. Much more research needs to be done.

But while we're waiting, here's something to consider. According to the Centers for Disease Control and Prevention, nearly one-quarter of adults and adolescents in the United States are infected with *T. gondii*. They just don't know it.

That means you…

…or someone you know…

…could be infected with a tiny, brain-dwelling zombie maker right now.

Remember: they're closer than you think.

ZOMBIE MAKERS: WHY AND HOW

Why do zombie makers go to so much trouble to invade and control their hosts? What's the point of their endless cycles of infection? The point is reproduction. All living things reproduce to make more of their own kind. If they didn't, they'd die out.

Reproduction isn't just about producing spores or eggs or some other type of offspring. It's also about doing things that give offspring the best chance to survive. By making their hosts act in ways they ordinarily wouldn't, zombie-making parasites greatly improve the odds that their offspring will carry on.

Ancient insects trapped in amber (fossilized tree sap) may hold clues about the history of nature's zombie makers.

Take the fly-enslaver fungus, *E. muscae*. Flies are a source of food for the fungus. But the fungus can also use them to travel to places more flies are likely to be. More flies mean more food—and hosts—for the fungus's spores. They give spores a better chance of successfully reproducing.

How does a fungus come to control a fly? How did any of these zombie makers develop the ability to manipulate their hosts as they do?

The best answer might be time.

All living things change, or evolve, over time. Given enough time, they can change a lot. Parasites and their hosts are engaged in a sort of war. A parasite invades. Its host fights back by developing better defenses. The parasite responds by coming up with new and better weapons. And on it goes, over millions of years.

How do we know? Fossils provide a few clues. Scientists have found tiny scars on 48-million-year-old leaf fossils. The scars look exactly like the marks that modern zombified carpenter ants make when they clamp onto leaves.

Scientists have also found a 105-million-year-old fossilized insect with fungus inside. Was that fungus a zombie maker? Perhaps. Or maybe it was on its way to becoming one.

Zombie makers are parasites with remarkably fine-tuned weapons. In most cases, these are chemicals that act on hosts' brains.

Exactly how this mind control works is still largely a mystery. Through experiments and new discoveries, though, scientists are finding answers. They're piecing together the amazing but true stories about nature's undead. About the real zombies—and their makers—that creep and crawl and lurk among us.

This is a fossil of a leaf that fell about 65 million years ago in New Zealand.

My inspiration to write this book came when I saw a photo of *Ophiocordyceps unilateralis* growing out of a carpenter ant's head and read how it came to be there. Mind control by a fungus—how deliciously creepy. Then I found dead houseflies stuck to my attic windows, each surrounded by a ring of spores. I had zombie makers in my own home!

Interacting with scientists who study zombie makers was the best part of researching this book. In phone conversations and e-mails, their excitement about their work always came through. I learned that several of these parasite-host relationships were discovered almost by accident. The discovery of worm-infested giant gliding ants by Steve Yanoviak and his colleagues started with a chance observation. Amir Grosman first noticed a caterpillar's zombie bodyguard behavior while raising caterpillars and the wasps that parasitize them. I also learned how dedicated the scientists are. One of David Hughes's graduate students, for instance, had an *O. unilateralis*-infected carpenter ant fall from the treetops directly onto her head. She spent the next hour on her hands and knees, following it through the forest undergrowth until it bit into a leaf.

Nature has no shortage of wonders. Scientists are finding new ones all the time. Even as I finished this book, a new zombie maker was discovered that infects honeybees. Who knows how many more are out there, just waiting to be found?

GLOSSARY

abdomen: the rear part of an insect's body

antenna: one in a pair of sense organs on the front of an insect's head that are used to feel things and, depending on the insect, to detect odors, humidity, and sounds

corpse: dead body

crustacean: an animal with a hard outer skeleton such as a crab, a shrimp, a barnacle, or a water flea. Most crustaceans live in water.

cyst: a small, rounded sac with a tough, protective outer wall in which a parasite spends a part of its life cycle

evolve: to change over time

fatal: deadly

gaster: the rounded, hindmost part of an ant's abdomen

host: a living plant or animal that has a parasite living in or on it

humidity: the amount of water, in gas form, in the air

larva: the young, wormlike feeding form of many insects that hatches from an egg and later changes into the adult form

life cycle: all the different stages in an organism's life, from the time it is born or hatches to adulthood when it reproduces to begin the cycle again

mate: to come together and breed to produce eggs or young that begin the next generation

mutate: to change into a new form

nerves: structures inside living things that carry information between the brain or spinal cord and the rest of the body

nervous system: the body system that carries messages for controlling movement and other functions between the brain and the rest of the body and includes the brain, spinal cord, and nerves

organ: a part of an animal or plant made up of cells and tissues that do a certain job. The heart, the lungs, and the kidneys are all organs.

parasite: an organism that lives in or on another organism called the host and gets its nutrients directly from it

protozoan: a microscopic, single-celled living thing that consumes other organisms for food and can move around on its own

pupal stage: a stage in the life cycle of certain insects in which a wormlike larva develops into a very different-looking adult form, usually inside a cocoon or similar structure. The form of the organism inside a cocoon is called a pupa.

reproduce: to produce new individuals of the same kind

saliva: the clear, watery liquid in the mouths of most animals

salivary gland: a structure in and in the back of the mouth that produces saliva

spore: a tiny reproductive structure similar to a seed made by fungi, ferns, mosses, and some other living things

tissue: a group of similar cells that work together

vaccine: a preparation, often made from a weakened disease-causing germ, that helps an organism fight off the disease caused by that germ and not get sick

venom: an often-poisonous substance that one animal injects into another through a bite or sting

virus: a small infectious agent that reproduces inside the cells of a living host and often causes disease

SOURCE NOTES

13 David Hughes, e-mail to the author, February 28, 2012.

29 Arne Janssen, e-mail to the author, February 17, 2012.

36 Steve Yanoviak, e-mail to the author, November 6, 2011.

41 Kevin Lafferty, e-mail to the author, February 13, 2012.

SELECTED BIBLIOGRAPHY

Andersen, Sandra B., Sylvia Gerritsma, Kalsum M. Yusah, David Mayntz, Nigel L. Hywel-Jones, Johan Billen, Jacobus J. Boomsma, and David P. Hughes. "The Life of a Dead Ant: The Expression of an Adaptive Extended Phenotype." *American Naturalist* 174, no. 3 (September 2009): 424–433.

Berdoy, M., J. P. Webster, and D. W. Macdonald. "Fatal Attraction in Rats Infected with *Toxoplasma gondii*." *Proceedings of the Royal Society of London* 267 (2000): 1,591–1,594.

Brahic, Catherine. "Zombie Caterpillars Controlled by Voodoo Wasps." *Newscientist.com*. June 4, 2008. http://www.newscientist.com/article/dn14053-zombie-caterpillars-controlled-by-voodoo-wasps.html (February 8, 2012).

Cain, Michael L., William D. Bowman, and Sally D. Hacker. "Parasitism." Chap. 13 in *Ecology*, 2nd ed. Sunderland, MA: Sinauer Associates, 2011. http://www.sinauer.com/ecology2e/Ecology2e_Ch13.pdf (February 8, 2012).

Carter Center. Guinea Worm Disease Eradication. 2012. http://www.cartercenter.org/health/guinea_worm/mini_site/index.html (February 8, 2012).

Gal, Ram, and Frederic Libersat. "A Wasp Manipulates Neuronal Activity in the Sub-Esophageal Ganglion to Decrease the Drive for Walking in Its Cockroach Prey." *PloS One* 5, no. 4, April 2010. http://www.plosone.org/article/info:doi%2F10.1371%2Fjournal.pone.0010019 (February 8, 2012).

Grosman, Amir H., Arne Janssen, Elaine F. de Brito, Eduardo G. Cordeiro, Felipe Colares, Juliana Oliveira Fonseca, Eraldo R. Lima, Angelo Pallini, and Maurice W. Sabelis. "Parasitoid Increases Survival of Its Pupae by Inducing Hosts to Fight Predators." *PloS One* 3, no. 6, June 2008. http://www.plosone.org/article/info:doi/10.1371/journal.pone.0002276 (February 8, 2012).

Hanelt, Ben, Matt Bolek, and Andreas Schmidt-Rhaesa. Hairworm Biodiversity Survey. 2012. http://www.nematomorpha.net/GeneralInformation.html (February 8, 2012).

Harmon, Katherine. "Zombie Creatures: What Happens When Animals Are Possessed by a Parasitic Puppet Master?" *Scientificamerican.com*. October 30, 2009. http://www.scientificamerican.com/slideshow.cfm?id=zombie-creatures-parasites (February 8, 2012).

Jones, Jeffrey L., Deanna Kruszon-Moran, Marianna Wilson, Geraldine McQuillan, Thomas Navin, and James B. McAuley. "*Toxoplasma gondii* Infection in the United States: Seroprevalence and Risk Factors." *American Journal of Epidemiology* 154, no. 4 (2001): 357–365.

Minard, Anne. "New, Fast-Evolving Rabies Virus Found—and Spreading." *National Geographic News*, May 4, 2009. http://news.nationalgeographic.com/news/2009/05/090504-rabies-evolution.html (February 8, 2012).

Nature Publishing Group. "How to Make a Zombie Cockroach." *Nature.com*. November 29, 2007. http://www.nature.com/news/2007/071129/full/news.2007.312.html (February 8, 2012).

Sanchez, Marta I., Fleur Ponton, Andreas Schmidt-Rhaesa, David P. Hughes, Dorothee Misse, and Frederic Thomas. "Two Steps to Suicide in Crickets Harbouring Hairworm." *Animal Behaviour* 76 (2008): 1,621–1,624.

ScienceDaily. "Zombie Ants Have Fungus on the Brain, New Research Reveals." *Sciencedaily.com*. May 9, 2011. http://www.sciencedaily.com/releases/2011/05/110509065536.htm (February 8, 2012).

Switek, Brian. "The Scariest Zombies in Nature." *Smithsonian.com*, October 18, 2010. http://www.smithsonianmag.com/science-nature/The-Scariest-Zombies-in-Nature.html (February 8, 2012).

Thomas, F., A. Schmidt-Rhaesa, G. Martin, C. Manu, P. Durand, and F. Renaud. "Do Hairworms (Nematomorpha) Manipulate the Water Seeking Behaviour of Their Terrestrial Hosts"? *Journal of Evolutionary Biology* 15 (2002): 356–361.

Tibayrenc, Michel, ed. *Encyclopedia of Infectious Diseases: Modern Methodologies*. Hoboken, NJ: Wiley-Liss, 2007.

Yanoviak, S. P., M. Kaspari, R. Dudley, and G. Poinar Jr. "Parasite-Induced Fruit Mimicry in a Tropical Canopy Ant." *American Naturalist* 171, no. 4 (April 2008): 536–544.

Yong, Ed. "The Wasp That Walks Cockroaches." *Discovermagazine.com*. June 5, 2008. http://blogs.discovermagazine.com/notrocketscience/2008/06/05/the-wasp-that-walks-cockroaches/ (February 8, 2012).

MORE TO EXPLORE

Websites and Videos

Ant Parasite Turns Host into Red Ripe Berry
http://www.berkeley.edu/news/media/releases/2008/01/ants-vid.shtml
Watch normal and zombie-maker-infected giant gliding ants in their treetop home.

Attack of the Killer Fungi
http://www.youtube.com/watch?v=XuKjBIBBAL8
Explore how zombie-making fungi invade, control, and destroy ants as well as a variety of other insects.

Hairworm Mind Control
http://www.youtube.com/watch?v=t778djMJiv8
In this short video, a zombie cockroach leaps into a swimming pool and its master—a hairworm—quickly emerges.

Jewel Wasps and Zombie Cockroaches
http://www.youtube.com/watch?v=qN2XMyxAs5o
This video takes you into a laboratory where scientists are studying how jewel wasps turn cockroaches into zombies—and food for their developing larvae.

Snail Zombies
http://www.youtube.com/watch?v=EWB_COSUXMw&feature=related
Follow the zombie-making worm *Leucochloridium paradoxum* from snail to bird and back again.

Zombie Caterpillar Controlled by Voodoo Wasps
http://www.youtube.com/watch?v=7UkDMrG6tog&feature=relmfu
This short video shows a zombie caterpillar in action as it stands guard over a cluster of wasp cocoons.

Books

Fleisher, Paul. *Parasites: Latching on to a Free Lunch*. Minneapolis: Twenty-First Century Books, 2006.

Klosterman, Lorrie. *Rabies*. New York: Marshall Cavendish Benchmark, 2008.

Marrin, Albert. *Little Monsters: The Creatures That Live on Us and in Us*. New York: Dutton Children's Books, 2011.

Mound, Laurence. *Insect*. London: New York: DK Pub., 2007.

Tilden, Thomasine E. Lewis. *Belly-Busting Worm Invasions! Parasites That Love Your Insides!* New York: Franklin Watts, 2008.

INDEX

PHOTO ACKNOWLEDGMENTS

The images in this book are used with the permission of: © AMC-TV/The Kobal Collection/Art Resource, NY, p. 5; © Donald Specker/Animals Animals, p. 7 (top); © Triarch/Visuals Unlimited, Inc., p. 7 (bottom); © Stanislav Krejcik, pp. 8–9 (top); © Heather Angel/Natural Visions, pp. 8–9 (bottom); © David P. Hughes, Ph.D., pp. 10 (both), 11, 12–13; © Andy Sands/naturepl.com, p. 15 (top); © Joel Sartore/National Geographic Stock, p. 15 (bottom); © Pascal Goetgheluck/Photo Researchers, Inc., pp. 16–17; AP Photo/John Bazemore, p. 18 (left); © Photononstop/SuperStock, p. 18 (right); © Spike Walker/Riser/Getty Images, p. 19; © Biophoto Associates/Photo Researchers, Inc., p. 20; © Charles O. Cecil/Alamy, p. 21; © Frank Greenaway/Dorling Kindersley/Getty Images, p. 23 (top); © Dorling Kindersley/Getty Images, p. 23 (middle); © Frank Greenaway/DK Limited/CORBIS, p. 23 (bottom); © Ram Gal, Ph.D., p. 24; © Biodiversity Institute of Ontario, p. 26 (left); © Amir Grosman, Ph.D., pp. 26 (right), 27, 28; © Chris Bjornberg/Photo Researchers, Inc., p. 31 (top); © Gail Shumway/Taxi/Getty Images, p. 31 (bottom); © Dietmar Nill/Minden Pictures, p. 32; © CNRI/Photo Researchers, Inc., p. 33; © Alex Wild/Visuals Unlimited, Inc., p. 35 (top); © George Poinar, Jr., Ph.D., p. 35 (bottom); © Stephen P. Yanoviak, Ph.D., p. 36 (both);© J. Meul-Van Cauteren/blickwinkel/Alamy, p. 37 (left); © Jeroen Stel/Peter Arnold/Getty Images, p. 37 (right); © Josef Hlasek, www.hlasek.com, p. 38; © Stephen Dalton/naturepl.com, p. 39 (left); © Moredun Scientific Ltd./Photo Researchers, Inc., p. 39 (right); © J.-L. Klein & M.-L. Hubert/Photo Researchers, Inc., p. 40; © Susumu Nishinaga/Photo Researchers, Inc., p. 41; © Thomas J. Abercrombie/National Geographic/Getty Images, p. 42; © Kenneth Garrett/National Geographic/Getty Images, p. 43.

Front cover: © Ram Gal, Ph.D. Front cover flap: © George Poinar, Jr., Ph.D. Back cover flap: © Kim Taylor/Minden Pictures.